# CHINESE
## ASTROLOGY

Understanding your horoscope

CHARTWELL
BOOKS

This edition published in 2015 by
CHARTWELL BOOKS
an imprint of Book Sales
a division of Quarto Publishing Group USA Inc.
276 Fifth Avenue Suite 206
New York, New York 10001
USA

Copyright © 2015 Amber Books Ltd.
74–77 White Lion Street
London N1 9PF
United Kingdom
www.amberbooks.co.uk

ISBN: 978-0-7858-3193-8

Translator: James Trapp
Project Editor: Sarah Uttridge
Design: Rick Rawcett
Illustrations: Amy Zhaoyue

Printed and bound in China

James Trapp took his degree in Chinese at SOAS, University of London,
specializing in Bronze Age art and archaeology and early Buddhist sculpture.
Until recently he was the China Education Manager at the British Museum
and currently works at the Confucius Institute at the Institute of Education,
University of London, promoting and supporting the study of Chinese in
English schools.

---

## TRADITIONAL CHINESE BOOKBINDING
This book has been produced using traditional Chinese bookbinding
techniques, using a method that was developed during the Ming Dynasty
(1368–1644) and remained in use until the adoption of Western binding
techniques in the early 1900s. In traditional Chinese binding, single sheets of
paper are printed on one side only, and each sheet is folded in half, with the
printed pages on the outside. The book block is then sandwiched between
two boards and sewn together through punched holes close to the cut edges
of the folded sheets.

# Introduction

At the Neolithic burial site of Xishuipo in Henan Province, North China, archaeologists excavated what many consider to be the first evidence of the Chinese fascination with astronomy and astrology. Dating to around 4000 BC, they found an adult male skeleton flanked by two mosaics made of white clam shells. One, to the east of the body, depicts a dragon, and the other, to the west, a tiger. At the skeleton's feet there is also a depiction of the constellation we call the Big Dipper, and that the Chinese know as 北斗 *běi dǒu*, the Northern Ladle. The popular explanation is that the body was that of a shaman laid out with the symbols of his connection to the powers of the cosmos. What seems beyond doubt is that these mosaics are the earliest instance of two of the Guardians of the Four Directions: the Azure Dragon of the East and the White Tiger of the West. Those two, along with their companions the Red Bird of the South and the Black Tortoise of the North, are an integral part of traditional Chinese astrological interpretation.

**The Heavens**
In the succeeding Bronze Age, particularly in the Shang Dynasty (sixteenth–eleventh centuries BC), we know that observations and interpretations of the movements of the heavens were of great importance to the ruling families. Inscriptions on bones used in divination, called oracle bones, record solar and lunar eclipses, comets, stars and star groups, and, of particular note, the planet Jupiter, 木星 *mù xīng*, the Wood Star. This is significant because the 12 years of the Earthly Branches and the Chinese zodiac are based on the observation of the time it took Jupiter to orbit the sun (11.86 years is the modern figure). Dates on oracle bones seldom if ever record years or months, but they do use the 60-day cycle of Heavenly Stems and Earthly Branches to record the days. The 10 Heavenly Stems were originally the names of the 10 days of the Shang week in accordance with the belief that there were 10 suns that appeared in succession.

The development of Chinese astrology may be seen as closely linked to the amalgamation of ancient belief systems, science and folk religion from which the philosophy of Daoism was formed. The nominal founder of Daoism, 老子 *Laozi*, is traditionally said to have lived during the sixth century BC, but it is not even certain that he actually existed, and the book attributed to him, 道德经 *Dào Dé Jīng*, is generally dated to the late fourth century. Whatever

# Contents

its origins, the development of Daoism, bringing together the theories of *yin* and *yang*, the Five Phases/Elements and other ancient cosmological understandings, is a central element of the flowering of religion and philosophy at that time. Briefly interrupted by the ruthless Legalism of Qin Shihuang, the First Emperor (221–210 BC), this golden age of Chinese thought continued in the Han Dynasty (206 BC–220 AD). It was in the Han Dynasty that many of the elements of Chinese astrology took the form that we recognize today.

The essential elements of Chinese astrology are the 60-year cycle formed from the ancient Heavenly Stems and Earthly Branches, and the various balances and counterpoints within this cycle of *yin* and *yang* and the Five Phases/Elements. These relate to the heavens through the astronomical classification of the constellations that form the 28 Mansions – calculated in relation to the cycle of the Moon. The 28 Mansions sub-divide into the four cardinal directions, each with its associated Guardian and Phase/Element. The 60-year cycle itself further divides into five 12-year cycles, in which each year has its corresponding zodiac animal. Horoscopes are read through the 八字 *bā zì*, eight Characters that represent the year, month, day and hour of birth according to the above divisions and principles. All of the above also have significant implications in the practice of Traditional Chinese Medicine and in feng shui.

## 12 Animals of the Zodiac

The element of Chinese astrology most familiar in the West is the 12 animals of the zodiac: Rat, Ox, Tiger, Rabbit, Dragon, Snake, Horse, Goat, Monkey, Rooster, Dog and Pig. This sequence is applied not just to the cycle of years, but to all the elements represented by the 8 Characters (see above); so one person may well be composed of different animal elements and influences. The precise origins of this sequence of animals are not known, but it became the established form during the Han Dynasty and various stories grew up about its origins in the mythical past. The most common of these is the story of the Great Race, ordered by the Jade Emperor, foremost of the ancient gods. Even within this there are many variations as to why the race was called in the first place, which animals competed and why they finished in the order they did. The one common feature is the victory of the quick-witted Rat, who tricks the Ox into carrying him across a river and then leaps to victory from the Ox's head. Other interesting elements include reasons for the absence of the Cat from the cycle, which also explains the permanent enmity between cats and rats and dogs.

# 12 Zodiac Animals

(SHÍ ÈR SHĒNG XIÀO)

The precise origins of the 12 animals of the Chinese zodiac are unclear, and are probably to be found in the combination of several systems and traditions. The use of the 12 Earthly Branches to represent periods of time across the cycles of years, months, days and hours was cemented in the Han Dynasty (206 BC–220 AD) and it is likely that the particular combination of animals familiar today was established then. There are several well-known mythical explanations too, particularly the race of the animals ordered by the Jade Emperor.

# Rat
## (SHǓ)

As with many of the animals of the Chinese zodiac, the rat does not carry the same connotations of character as in Western tradition. Rats, as befits the animal that won the race (see introduction) have vitality, wit, alertness and adaptability. On the downside, they can be timid, stubborn, volatile and selfish. Rats are best matched with Dragons, Monkeys and Oxen; they should avoid Horses and Rabbits. The Rat is a *yang* sign associated with the Water element.

*Famous Rats: George Washington, Shakespeare, Prince Charles, Cameron Diaz*

# Ox
(NIÚ)

The Ox's characteristics are similar in both Chinese and Western tradition. Oxen are larger-than-life, honest, straightforward and persistent. Even their character flaws are not too bad: they can be taciturn, not good at expressing thoughts and feelings and stubborn. Overall, they are conservative and great respecters of tradition and family values. Their best matches are Rats, Snakes and Roosters; they should avoid Horses, Dogs and Goats. The Ox is a *yin* sign associated with the Water element.

*Famous Oxen: Napoleon, Walt Disney, Barack Obama, Kiera Knightley*

# Tiger
## (HǓ)

The tiger was the symbol of the emperor in ancient China, and this
sign is associated with both the good and the bad characteristics
of powerful rulers. On the plus side, Tigers are strong, fearless,
chivalrous and worthy of respect. On the other hand, they can be short-
tempered, high-handed, rash and even untrustworthy in their own
interests. Tigers match Horses and Dogs, and should avoid Snakes and
Monkeys. The Tiger is a *yang* sign associated with the Wood element.

*Famous Tigers: Beethoven, Eisenhower, Marilyn Monroe,*
*Beatrix Potter*

# Rabbit
## (TÚ)

Rabbits have an important place in Chinese mythology, including the rabbit who lives on the Moon with the goddess Chang-e. In astrology, Rabbits are compassionate, modest, gentle and kind. Their faults, such as they are, are a tendency to escapism and to place romance over reality; they can be stubborn through lack of forward-thinking. Rabbits suit Sheep, Pigs and Dogs; they should avoid Rats and Dragons. The Rabbit is a *yin* sign associated with the Wood element.

*Famous Rabbits: Queen Victoria, Albert Einstein, Angelina Jolie, David Beckham*

# Dragon
## (LÓNG)

The Dragon is the most powerful and auspicious of the zodiac animals.
Married couples in China may delay trying for a child until they
can be sure it will be born in a Dragon year. Dragons are energetic,
ambitious and straightforward but also inclined to arrogance,
intolerance and unpredictability. Dragons match well with Rats,
Monkeys and Roosters, but should avoid Oxen, Rabbits and Dogs. The
Dragon is a *yang* sign associated with the Wood element.

*Famous Dragons: Joan of Arc, Florence Nightingale, Sigmund Freud,
Russell Crowe*

# Snake
### (SHÉ)

The Snake is an enigmatic sign, with characteristics that can express themselves equally for good or bad. As in the West, it can symbolize evil, yet at New Year, a snake twining round a rabbit is a symbol of good fortune. Snakes can be wise, passionate, highly moral, and sympathetic, but also moody, jealous and suspicious. Snakes should seek out Dragons, Oxen and Roosters but especially avoid Pigs. The Snake is a *yin* sign associated with the Fire element.

*Famous Snakes: Abraham Lincoln, Mahatma Gandhi, Martin Luther King, Audrey Hepburn*

# Horse
## (MĂ)

The horse has been an animal of great importance and significance throughout Chinese history, and the sign of the Horse is seen as representing the power and endurance of the Chinese people. Horses are cheerful, talented, public-spirited and determined. They can also be impatient, pig-headed and with a tendency to attention-seeking. Horses match well with Goats, Dogs and Tigers but should avoid Rats and Oxen. The Horse is a *yang* sign associated with the Fire element.

*Famous Horses: Genghis Khan, Chopin, Aretha Franklin, John Travolta*

# Goat
## (YÁNG)

The Chinese character does not differentiate between sheep and goat. This is a gentle sign and even its bad points are weaknesses rather than faults. Goats are clever, sensitive, artistic and wise. They are very family-oriented. On the flip-side, they can be needy, shy, pessimistic and unable to make decisions for themselves. The best partners for Goats are Horses, Rabbits, Pigs and Dragons, but they should steer clear of Oxen. The Goat is a *yin* sign associated with the Fire element.

*Famous Goats: Michelangelo, Thomas Edison, Muhammad Ali, Julia Roberts*

# Monkey
## (HÓU)

The Monkey's character is most fully illustrated in Sun Wukong, the mischievously heroic Monkey King of the classic novel, *The Journey to the West*. Monkeys are quick-witted, confident and capable, but, like Snakes, they can lapse into moodiness, jealousy and suspicion. Impatience may get in the way of their natural creativity. Snakes, Dragons and Rats all get on well with Monkeys, but, not surprisingly, Monkeys and Tigers do not mix. The Monkey is a *yang* sign associated with the Metal element.

*Famous Monkeys: Julius Caesar, Leonardo da Vinci, Charles Dickens, Miley Cyrus*

# Rooster
## (JĪ)

With Roosters, what you see is what you get. They are vain about their appearance, but upright, honest, able and good communicators. They can be impatient with others, and may be critical and volatile. Their self-confidence can turn into pomposity, but overall their heart is in the right place and their eccentricity is easily forgiven. Roosters match well with Dragons, Snakes and Oxen, but should avoid Rabbits and Rats. The Rooster is a *yin* sign associated with the Metal element.

*Famous Roosters: Catherine the Great, Groucho Marx,*
*Roger Federer, Jennifer Aniston*

# Dog
## (GǑU)

There are pottery models of watch-dogs excavated in China from the third century BC, so we know the virtues of the dog have long been prized there. Dogs are courageous, clever, steady and loyal. Female Dogs, however, may have a tendency to stand-offishness and are not always kind to other people's reputations. Dogs match well with Rabbits, Tigers and Horses, but should avoid Dragons and Oxen. The Dog is a *yang* sign associated with the Metal element.

*Famous Dogs: Socrates, Benjamin Franklin, Madonna, Michael Jackson*

# Pig
## (ZHŪ)

The Chinese character for home shows a pig under a roof, illustrating
the importance of this animal throughout history. Pigs may not be
as quick-witted as dogs, but they are deep thinkers. They are honest,
sincere and loyal. They may also be quick-tempered and too trusting.
Pigs may be a little too fond of material possessions. Pigs should seek
out Goats, Rabbits and Tigers, but absolutely avoid Snakes. The Pig is
a *yin* sign associated with the Water element.

*Famous Pigs: Henry VIII, Arnold Schwarzenegger, Hillary Clinton,*
*Julie Andrews*

# 12 Earthly Branches

(SHÍ ÈR DÌ ZHĪ)

The 12 Earthly Branches are used in combination with the 10 Heavenly Stems to create the 60-year cycle of the traditional Chinese calendar. The Branches probably pre-date the Stems, but both were certainly in use in the Bronze Age Shang Dynasty (sixteenth–eleventh centuries BC), although not in combination. The 12 Branches are based on ancient observations of the orbit of the planet Jupiter, known both as 木星 *mù xīng,* the Wood Star, and as 歲星 *suì xīng,* the Year Star. The Heavenly Stems are a vital element of the 八字 *bā zì* horoscope system.

# Zǐ

子 is the first of the 12 Earthly Branches and corresponds with 鼠 the Rat in the animal zodiac. It therefore shares the same characteristics of being a *yang* Branch associated with the Water element. It can only pair with Heavenly Stems that are also *yang* and occurs as the 1st, 13th, 25th, 37th and 49th years of the 60-year cycle. It represents the first of the twelve 2-hour divisions of the day, 2300–0100. Its season is winter and its direction is 0° north.

# Chǒu

丑 is the second of the 12 Earthly Branches and corresponds
with 牛 the Ox in the animal zodiac. It therefore shares the same
characteristics of being a *yin* Branch associated with the Water
element. It can only pair with Heavenly Stems that are also *yin* and
occurs as the 2nd, 14th, 26th, 38th and 50th years of the 60-year cycle.
It represents the second of the twelve 2-hour divisions of the day,
01.00–03.00. Its season is winter and its direction is 30° northeast.

# Yín

寅 is the third of the 12 Earthly Branches and corresponds with 虎 the Tiger in the animal zodiac. It therefore shares the same characteristics of being a *yang* Branch associated with the Wood element. It can only pair with Heavenly Stems that are also *yang* and occurs as the 3rd, 15th, 27th, 39th and 51st years of the 60-year cycle. It represents the third of the twelve 2 hour divisions of the day, 0300–0500. Its season is spring and its direction is 60° northeast.

# Mǎo

卯 is the fourth of the 12 Earthly Branches and corresponds with
兔 the Rabbit in the animal zodiac. It therefore shares the same
characteristics of being a *yin* Branch associated with the Wood
element. It can only pair with Heavenly Stems that are also *yin* and
occurs as the 4th, 16th, 28th, 40th and 52nd years of the 60-year cycle.
It represents the fourth of the twelve 2-hour divisions of the day,
0500–0700. Its season is spring and its direction is 90° east.

# Chén

辰 is the fifth of the 12 Earthly Branches and corresponds with 龍 the Dragon in the animal zodiac. It therefore shares the same characteristics of being a *yang* Branch associated with the Wood element. It can only pair with Heavenly Stems that are also *yang* and occurs as the 5th, 17th, 29th, 41st and 53rd years of the 60-year cycle. It represents the fifth of the twelve 2-hour divisions of the day, 0700–0900. Its season is spring and its direction is 120° southeast.

# Sì

巳 is the sixth of the 12 Earthly Branches and corresponds with 蛇 the Snake in the animal zodiac. It therefore shares the same characteristics of being a *yin* Branch associated with the Fire element. It can only pair with Heavenly Stems that are also *yin* and occurs as the 6th, 18th, 30th, 42nd and 54th years of the 60-year cycle. It represents the sixth of the twelve 2-hour divisions of the day, 0900–1100. Its season is summer and its direction is 150° southeast.

# Wǔ

午 is the seventh of the 12 Earthly Branches and corresponds with 馬 the Horse in the animal zodiac. It therefore shares the same characteristics of being a *yang* Branch associated with the Fire element. It can only pair with Heavenly Stems that are also *yang* and occurs as the 7th, 19th, 31st, 43rd and 55th years of the 60-year cycle. It represents the seventh of the twelve 2-hour divisions of the day, 1100–1300. Its season is summer and its direction is 180° south.

# Wèi

未 is the eighth of the 12 Earthly Branches and corresponds with
羊 the Goat in the animal zodiac. It therefore shares the same
characteristics of being a *yin* Branch associated with the Fire
element. It can only pair with Heavenly Stems that are also *yin* and
occurs as the 8th, 20th, 32nd, 44th and 56th years of the 60-year
cycle. It represents the eighth of the twelve 2-hour divisions of the
day, 1300–1500. Its season is summer and its direction is
210° southwest.

# Shēn

申 is the ninth of the 12 Earthly Branches and corresponds with
猴 the Monkey in the animal zodiac. It therefore shares the same
characteristics of being a *yang* Branch associated with the Metal
element. It can only pair with Heavenly Stems that are also *yang* and
occurs as the 9th, 21st, 33rd, 45th and 57th years of the 60-year cycle.

It represents the ninth of the twelve 2-hour divisions of the day,
1500–1700. Its season is autumn and its direction is 240° southwest.

# Yǒu

酉 is the tenth of the 12 Earthly Branches and corresponds with 雞 the Rooster in the animal zodiac. It therefore shares the same characteristics of being a *yin* Branch associated with the Metal element. It can only pair with Heavenly Stems that are also *yin* and occurs as the 10th, 22nd, 34th, 46th and 58th years of the 60-year cycle. It represents the tenth of the twelve 2 hour divisions of the day, 1700–1900. Its season is autumn and its direction is 270° west.

# Xū

戌 is the eleventh of the 12 Earthly Branches and corresponds with 狗 the Dog in the animal zodiac. It therefore shares the same characteristics of being a *yang* Branch associated with the Metal element. It can only pair with Heavenly Stems that are also *yang* and occurs as the 11th, 23rd, 35th, 47th and 59th years of the 60-year cycle. It represents the eleventh of the twelve 2-hour divisions of the day, 1900–2100. Its season is autumn and its direction is 300° northwest.

# Hài

亥 is the twelfth of the 12 Earthly Branches and corresponds
with 豬 the Pig in the animal zodiac. It therefore shares the same
characteristics of being a *yin* Branch associated with the Water
element. It can only pair with Heavenly Stems that are also *yin* and
occurs as the 12th, 24th, 36th, 48th and 60th years of the 60-year cycle.
It represents the twelfth of the twelve 2-hour divisions of the day,
2100–2300. Its season is winter and its direction is 330° northwest.

# Five Phases

## (WǓ XÌNG)

The Five Phases, also commonly referred to as the Five Elements, are 木 *mù*, Wood, 火 *huǒ*, Fire, 土 *tǔ*, Earth, 金 *jīn*, Metal and 水 *shuǐ*, Water. In that order they form two interdependent cycles of mutual generation and destruction that are fundamental to the understanding of traditional Chinese science, medicine and belief. They embody the guiding principles of both the natural order of the cosmos and of human life, health and behaviour. Like the 12 zodiac animals, they were shaped into this form from aspects of older traditions during the Han Dynasty (206 BC–220 AD).

# Wood
## (MÙ)

木 is the first phase of the 五行 *wǔ xìng*, the Five Phases. It represents the east, the season spring and the planet Jupiter. Its colour is green/blue and within the 28 Mansions into which Chinese astronomy divides the heavens, it is represented by the seven stars that form the Azure Dragon. It is associated with growth and generation. It interacts positively with Water and Fire, and destructively with Earth and Metal. In Traditional Chinese Medicine it is the element of the liver and the gall bladder. Its life-phase is birth and it is rising *yang*.

# East
## (DŌNG)

East is the direction of the Wood phase. It is associated with 兔 *tù*, the Rabbit, the Earthly Branch 卯 *máo*, and the Celestial Stems 甲 *jiǎ* and 乙 *yǐ*. The East phase is that of spring, birth and new growth. In 风水 *fēng shuǐ* the East is the area of health and family harmony, but it is not an area recommended for sleeping. Its colours are blue/green and brown. The Guardian of the Four Directions associated with the East is the Azure Dragon.

# Spring
## (CHŪN)

Spring is the season associated with the Wood phase. It is the season
that sees *yang* on the rise after the full *yin* aspect of the deep winter
months. As in most other traditions, it is the season of rebirth and
growth. 春节 *chūn jié*, the Spring Festival that marks the Chinese
Lunar New Year, is the most important celebration in both the
traditional and the modern calendar. The festival lasts 15 days and
is the time when families dispersed across China and the rest of the
world return to their ancestral homes.

# Azure Dragon
## (QĪNG LÓNG)

The Azure Dragon of the East is one of the Guardians of the Four Directions, also known as 四象 *sì xiàng* the Four Symbols. You can see a tomb tile from the Eastern Han Dynasty (25–220 AD) here: *http://www.asianart.com/exhibitions/shandong/28.html*. The Azure Dragon represents the Wood element and the season spring. In Daoist tradition it has the human name 孟章 *Mèng Zhāng*. Astronomically and astrologically it is composed of the seven stars east of the path of the Moon as the eastern part of the 28 Mansions. It is also known as the Green Dragon.

# Jupiter
## (MÙ XĪNG)

木星 literally translates as Wood Star and even in current usage is still the Chinese name for the planet Jupiter. It is of particular significance in Chinese astrology and astronomy since the divisions of the 12-year cycle were based on ancient observations of its orbit. It carries with it themes of strength and steadfastness as well as the qualities of patience and compassion.

# Green

## (LÜ)

This character 绿 *lü* is more directly translatable as 'green' than the
character 青 in 青龍 *qīng lóng*, the Azure Dragon, also called the
Green Dragon. 青 covers a spectrum of colours between green and
blue. Green, in the context of Chinese astrology, is an auspicious
colour representing spring, birth and regrowth. However, in popular
tradition even today, it is the colour of marital infidelity. Gifts that
contain green are considered an insult as they suggest that a male
recipient is being cheated on by his partner.

# Liver
## (GĀN)

The liver is one of the two 臟腑 *zàng fǔ* (principal organs)
associated in Traditional Chinese Medicine with the Wood phase.
The other is the gallbladder (see 膽 opposite). The liver is the *yin*
organ of the pair. The liver is pivotal to the overall harmonious
functioning of the body as it regulates and facilitates the flow of
vital energy 氣 *qì*. Its physical function is reflected in its role in
maintaining harmonious emotions, and malfunction in the liver
results in excess heat and therefore anger.

# Gallbladder
## (DǍN)

The gallbladder is one of the two 臟 腑 *zàng fǔ* (principal organs) associated in Traditional Chinese Medicine with the Wood phase. The other is the liver (see 肝 opposite). The gallbladder is the *yang* organ of the pair. It is the storage organ for excess heat (*yang*) and dampness (*yin*) and one of its principal functions is to absorb any results of imbalance in the liver. In the emotions, it controls the balance between decisiveness and timidity. Overall, it governs the right side of the body.

.

# Fire
## (HUǑ)

火 is the second phase of the 五行 *wǔ xìng*, the five Phases. It represents the south, the season summer and the planet Mars. Its colour is red and within the 28 Mansions into which Chinese astronomy divides the heavens, it is represented by the seven stars that form the Vermilion Bird. It is associated with swelling and ripening. It interacts positively with Wood and Earth, and destructively with Water and Metal. In Traditional Chinese Medicine it is the element of the heart and the small intestine. Its life-phase is youth and it is full *yang*.

# South

## (NÁN)

South is the direction of the Fire phase. It is associated with 馬 *mǎ* the Horse, the Earthly Branch 午 *wǔ*, and the Celestial Stems 丙 *bǐng* and 丁 *dīng*. The South phase is that of summer, and fulfilment of the potential of new growth in spring. In 风水 *fēng shuǐ* the South is the area of fame and reputation and realization of inner potential. Its primary colour is red, but green is also good since Wood nourishes Fire. The Guardian of the Four Directions associated with the South is the Vermilion Bird.

# Summer

### (XIÀ)

Summer is the season associated with the Fire phase. It is the season that sees *yang* at its height, building on the burgeoning *yang* of spring. This is a season of warmth, activity and abundance. 黄帝內經 *Huángdì Nèijīng, The Yellow Emperor's Inner Canon*, the early medical text composed sometime between fifth–first century BC, states that during summer one should stay physically active and try to avoid anger. To ensure the free flow of energy 氣 one should let go of grudges and look to be happy and easygoing.

# Vermilion Bird

## (ZHŪ QUÈ)

The Vermilion Bird of the South is one of the Guardians of the Four Directions, also known as 四象 *sì xiàng*, the Four Symbols. You can see a tomb tile from the E Han Dynasty (25–220 AD) here: *http:// www.asianart.com/exhibitions/shandong/30.html*. The Vermilion Bird represents the Fire element and the season summer. It is a *yang* element. Astronomically and astrologically it is composed of the seven stars south of the path of the Moon as the southern part of the 28 Mansions. It is also known as the Red Bird.

# Mars
## (HUǑ XĪNG)

火星 literally translates as Fire Star and even in current usage is still the Chinese name for the planet Mars. Known in many cultures as the Red Planet, the Chinese association of Mars with Fire is an obvious one. In mythology it is the home of Xie Tianjun, a red-faced warrior god who also governs the summer. Mars' energy is vigorous, passionate and adventurous.

# Red
## (HÓNG)

In the hierarchy of colours in Chinese symbolism, the yellow of the Earth Phase may rank highest, but the red of Fire is by far the most popular and ubiquitous. It is the lucky colour for every occasion. In the mythology of the Chinese New Year it was used to scare away the evil monster Nian. It is inextricably associated not just with that festival, but with all celebrations. Its symbolism has also been incorporated into the national flag of the People's Republic of China.

# Heart

## (XĪN)

The heart is one of the two 臟腑 *zàng fǔ* (principal organs) associated in Traditional Chinese Medicine with the Fire phase. The other is the small intestine (see小腸 opposite). The heart is the *yin* organ of the pair. In fact, 心 here does not refer just to the heart but to the whole circulatory system. The heart is the ruler of the body and governs the circulation of both blood and 氣 *qì* energy. The circulatory vessels also house 神 *shén*, spirit, the immaterial essence of change that governs the actions of the material body.

# Small Intestine
## (XIǍO CHÁNG)

The small intestine is one of the two 臟腑 *zàng fǔ* (principal organs) associated in Traditional Chinese Medicine with the Fire phase. The other is the heart (see 心 opposite). The small intestine is the *yang* organ of the pair. It is responsible for receiving nourishment matured in the stomach and separating it into its pure and impure essences. The pure essences are circulated through the body via the spleen, and the impure passed on to the large intestine for elimination. Imbalances in the small intestine cause anxiety and agitation.

51

# Earth
## (TŬ)

土 is the third phase of the 五行 *wǔ xìng*, the Five Phases. It represents
the Middle, the four 18-day periods of change between seasons and
the planet Saturn. Its colour is yellow or orange. Its Guardian is the
Yellow Dragon, but, as the Middle, it does not have a corresponding
constellation. It is associated with stabilizing and harmonizing. It
interacts positively with Metal and destructively with Water. It is the
element of the spleen and the stomach. Its life-phase is maturity and it
is the balancing point of *yin* and *yang*.

# Middle
## (ZHŌNG)

中 Middle is the direction of the Earth phase. It is associated with
龍 *lóng*, the Dragon, the Earthly Branch 辰 *chén* , and the Celestial
Stems 戊 *wù* and 己 *jǐ*. The Middle phase is that of maturity and
consolidation. In 风水 *fēng shuǐ* the Middle is the area of spiritual
growth and self-cultivation, but it is not an area recommended for
children's rooms. Its colours are orange/yellow and light brown. The
Guardian of the Four Directions associated with the Middle is the
Yellow Dragon.

# Change of Season
## (JÌ)

The Earth phase is one of maturing and it does not have a single season associated with it. Some traditions have it representing just the end of summer; but more commonly, as befits its balance of *yin* and *yang*, it is taken to represent the periods of change in the cycle of the seasons. Balance and smooth transition are concepts central to Daoist belief and also, particularly, to Traditional Chinese Medicine. In this context the change of seasons can also be taken to refer to periods of change in all aspects of human existence.

# Yellow Dragon
## (HUÁNG LÓNG)

The Yellow Dragon of the Middle is a later addition to the Guardians
of the Four Directions, 四象 *sì xiàng*, the Four Symbols introduced
to align them with the Five Phases. It is seldom represented in early
depictions of the Guardians. The Yellow Dragon represents the Earth
phase and the periods between the seasons. It has symbolic meaning
that goes well beyond the Five Phases and Directions; the mythical
founder of the Chinese people, the Yellow Emperor, is said to have
transformed himself into a yellow dragon, and this also became the
symbol of the Chinese emperors.

# Saturn
## (TǓ XĪNG)

土星 literally translates as Earth Star and even in current usage is
still the Chinese name for the planet Saturn. As befits the planet at the
balancing point of *yin* and *yang* it carries with it themes of warmth,
solidarity and co-operation as well as the qualities of responsibility
and reliability. The beige/yellow colour of the planet itself is reflected
in the association of yellow with the Earth phase.

# Yellow
## (HUÁNG)

Yellow is a fundamentally important colour in Chinese tradition – even more important than the lucky colour red (see 火 Fire). The Yellow Emperor is the legendary founder of Chinese civilization, and from myth into reality, at least from the Han Dynasty (206 BC–220 AD) onwards, yellow has been the colour of imperial power. From the Ming Dynasty (1368–1644 AD) onwards it was exclusively reserved for use by the imperial court, and the red walls of the Forbidden City are topped with yellow roofs.

# Spleen
### (PÍ)

The spleen is one of the two 臟腑 *zàng fǔ* (principal organs) associated
in Traditional Chinese Medicine with the Earth phase. The other
is the stomach (see 胃 opposite). The spleen is the *yin* organ of the
pair. Unlike Western understanding of the function of this organ, in
Traditional Chinese Medicine the spleen works in partnership with the
stomach to absorb and process nutrition and to maintain the body's
strength. It also governs the blood and fluid metabolism. The 'upright
*qi*' of the spleen holds the other organs in their correct positions.

# Stomach

## (WÈI)

The stomach is one of the two 臟腑 *zàng fǔ* (principal organs) associated in Traditional Chinese Medicine with the Earth phase. The other is the spleen (see 脾 opposite). The stomach is the *yang* organ of the pair. In Traditional Chinese Medicine it is viewed as the cauldron in which food cooked and ripened for processing by the spleen. It has 'downward *qi*', which ensures the correct movement of nutrition through the digestive system. Deficiency in both the spleen and the stomach causes anxiety and stress.

# Metal

## (JĪN)

金 is the fourth phase of the 五行 *wǔ xìng*, the Five Phases. It represents the West, the season autumn and the planet Venus. Its colour is white or silver and within the 28 Mansions into which Chinese astronomy divides the heavens, it is represented by the seven stars that form the White Tiger. It is associated with contracting and withering. It interacts positively with Water and Earth, and negatively with Wood and Fire. In Traditional Chinese Medicine it is the element of the large intestine and the respiratory system. Its life-phase is old age and it is rising *yin*.

# West

## (XĪ)

West is the direction of the Metal phase. It is associated with 雞 *jī* the Rooster, the Earthly Branch 酉 *yǒu*, and the Celestial Stems 庚 *gēng* and 辛 *xīn*. The West phase is that of autumn, and decline. In 风水 *fēng shuǐ* the South is the area of creativity, career development and the energy of children. Its primary colour is white, but silver and bright metallic colours are also good. Crystals are at their most potent in the West area of your house or office. The Guardian of the Four Directions associated with the West is the White Tiger.

# Autumn

## (QIŪ)

Autumn is the season associated with the Metal phase. It sees *yin* on the rise after the period of *yin–yang* balance in the summer. It is a period of old age and decline, but also, of course, of harvesting and collecting. The second most important festival of the traditional calendar, 中秋節 *Zhōngqiū Jié*, the Mid-Autumn Festival or Moon Festival, falls in this period. Its origins as a harvest festival go back to the Shang Dynasty (sixteenth–eleventh century BC), but in modern times it is primarily associated with the Moon and romance.

# White Tiger
## (BÁI HǓ)

The White Tiger of the West is one of the Guardians of the Four Directions, also known as 四象 *sì xiàng* the Four Symbols. You can see a tomb tile from the Eastern Han Dynasty (25–220 AD) here: *http://www.asianart.com/exhibitions/shandong/29.html*. The White Tiger represents the Metal element and the season autumn. In Daoist tradition it has the human name 監兵 *Jiān Bīng*. Astronomically and astrologically it is composed of the seven stars east of the path of the Moon as the eastern part of the 28 Mansions.

# Venus

## (JĪN XĪNG)

金星 literally translates as 'Metal Planet' and even in current usage is still the Chinese name for the planet Venus. The association with aspects of the Metal phase is both in its white metallic colour, and its rising in the west as the morning star. Conversely to Western tradition, Venus is a very masculine planet in Chinese symbolism, and brings, with its metallic nature, qualities of forcefulness and obduracy. Metal as the material for agricultural implements and weapons reinforces this association.

# White
## (BÁI)

White, because it is plain and unadorned, is the traditional colour
of mourning in China, but despite this it is a positive colour in other
aspects. The character 金 means not just 'metal', but also 'gold' and
by extension 'money'. Its associated colour, therefore, also represents
prosperity and success. It can also share the Western characteristics of
purity. In *feng shui* it is a colour of *yang* energy and creativity. It is a
good colour for areas concerned with the well-being of children.

# Respiratory System
## (FÈI)

The lungs are one of the two 臟腑 *zàng fǔ* (principal organs)
associated in Traditional Chinese Medicine with the Metal phase. The
other is the large intestine (see 大肠 opposite). The lungs are the *yin*
organ of the pair. Their most important function is as the guardian at
the point of contact between the interior and the exterior worlds. They
govern the exchange of incoming pure air *qi* and outgoing depleted
body *qi* and their dominating energy affects all the functions of the
body. The lungs are the organ of grief.

# Large Intestine
## (DÀ CHÁNG)

The large intestine is one of the two 臟腑 *zàng fǔ* (principal organs) associated in Traditional Chinese Medicine with the Metal phase. The other is the lungs (see 肺 opposite). The large intestine is the *yang* organ of the pair. As is often the case in Traditional Chinese Medicine, it is more an energy system than an anatomically definable organ as it is in Western medicine. Proper functioning of the large intestine is closely linked to emotional well-being, upon which any blockages may have adverse effects such as depression or obsession.

# Water
## (SHUǏ)

水 is the fifth and final phase of the 五行 *wǔ xìng*, the Five Phases. It represents the north, the season winter and the planet Mercury. Its colours are black and grey, and within the 28 Mansions into which Chinese astronomy divides the heavens, it is represented by the seven stars that form the Black Tortoise. It is associated with dormancy and death. It interacts positively with Wood and Metal, and destructively with Earth and Fire. In Traditional Chinese Medicine it is the element of the urinary and skeletal systems. Its life-phase is death and it is full *yin*.

# North
## (BĚI)

North is the direction of the Water phase. It is associated with 鼠 *shǔ*, the Rat, the Earthly Branch 子 *zǐ*, and the Celestial Stems 壬 *rén* and 癸 *guǐ*. The North phase is that of winter, death and dormancy. In 风水 *fēng shuǐ* the North is the area of career and life path and is a good place for a home office. Its colours are deep blue, grey and black. The Guardian of the Four Directions associated with the East is the Black Tortoise.

# Winter
## (DŌNG)

Winter is the season associated with the Water phase. It is the season of full *yin* after the transitional season of autumn. It is a time of stillness in nature when deep underlying energies are replenished and it nurtures the potential for rebirth and regrowth. Of lesser importance nowadays than the Spring Festival, 冬至 *dōng zhì*, the Winter Solstice that coincides approximately with Christmas, is still a significant festival when families gather to mark the beginning of the new cycle. It is a time for optimism.

# Black Tortoise
## (XUÁN WǓ)

The Black Tortoise of the North is one of the Guardians of the Four Directions, also known as 四象 *sì xiàng*, the Four Symbols. You can see a tomb tile from the Eastern Han Dynasty (25–220 AD) here: *http://www.asianart.com/exhibitions/shandong/31.html*. The Black Tortoise represents the Water element and the season winter. It shares its name with the Daoist god 玄武 *Xuán Wǔ*. It is composed of the seven stars north of the path of the Moon as the northern part of the 28 Mansions. It is also known as the Black Warrior.

# Mercury

## (SHUǏ XĪNG)

水星 literally translates as 'Water Star' and even in current usage is still the Chinese name for the planet Mercury. Mercury's associations are intelligence, diplomacy and communication, of which the latter has interesting resonances with the Western classical Mercury as the messenger of the gods. In ancient China it was also known as 辰星 *chén xīng*, the Hour Star or Morning Star.

# Black

## (HĒI)

Black is the colour of the Water phase, and as befits the nature of its element, its symbolism is diffuse and hard to pin down. In the most ancient Chinese beliefs it was the colour of heaven and of 天帝 *tiān dì* supreme ruler of the cosmos. It is also the colour used in Daoist philosophy to represent the *yin* principle in the *yin–yang* continuum. Despite, or perhaps because of, the power it embodies, black also spills over into many of the negative associations of death, evil and corruption that it carries in the West.

# Kidney
(SHÈN)

The kidney is one of the two 臟腑 *zàng fǔ* (principal organs)
associated in Traditional Chinese Medicine with the Water phase.
It is to be taken as referring to the system that incorporates the two
kidneys, rather than an individual organ. The other Water organ is
the urinary bladder (see 胱 opposite). The kidney is the *yin* organ of
the pair, although as a pair, the kidneys represent both *yin* and *yang*.
It is fundamental to human life as it is the storage organ for 精 *jīng*,
the essence of 氣 *qì*, vital energy.

# Bladder
## (GUĀNG)

The bladder is one of the two 臟腑 *zàng fǔ* (principal organs)
associated in Traditional Chinese Medicine with the Water phase. The
other is the kidney (see 腎 opposite). The bladder is the *yang* organ
of the pair. The bladder's role is that of a minister or civil official
receiving impure liquids from the small intestine, processing them
into urine and organizing their excretion. Imperfect bladder function
may result in irrational fear, suspicion and even moral degeneracy.
The bladder is also closely linked to the efficient functioning of the
autonomous nervous system.

75

# 10 Heavenly Stems

(SHÍ TIĀN GĀN)

The 10 Heavenly Stems are used in combination with the 12 Earthly Branches to create the 60-year cycle of the traditional Chinese calendar. In the Bronze Age Shang Dynasty (sixteenth century– eleventh century BC) there was a belief that there were 10 suns that appeared in turn in a 10-day cycle, and the Heavenly Stems were the names given to these suns. They were also used in the generational names of the ruling family. The Heavenly Stems are a vital element of the 八字 *bā zì* horoscope system.

# 1st Heavenly Stem
## (JIĂ)

甲 is the *yang* stem of the 甲 *jiǎ* 乙 *yǐ* pair associated with the Wood
element. In the 八字 *bā zì* horoscope system its characteristics are
direct, stern and may be unimaginative and lacking in empathy. It
represents a natural conservatism and reluctance to change but also
determination and steadfastness.

# 2nd Heavenly Stem
## (YǏ)

乙 is the *yin* stem of the 甲 *jiǎ* 乙 *yǐ* pair associated with the Wood element. In the 八字 *bā zì* horoscope system its characteristics are the opposite of 甲, showing adaptability and flexibility. Its ability to change according to circumstances has short-term advantages that may dissolve into inconstancy and unreliability.

# 3rd Heavenly Stem
## (BĬNG)

丙 is the *yang* stem of the 丙 *bǐng* 丁 *dīng* pair associated with the
Fire element. In the 八字 *bā zì* horoscope system its characteristics
are warmth, vibrancy and generosity. It can, however, be subverted by
self-obsession and attachment to routine, but is always open and free
of subterfuge.

# 4th Heavenly Stem
## (DĪNG)

丁 is the *yin* stem of the 丙 *bǐng* 丁 *dīng* pair associated with the Fire element. In the 八字 *bā zì* horoscope system its characteristics are of leadership and the ability to inspire. Conversely these effects on others may find a negative expression in relation to the self, resulting in loss of purpose and motivation.

# 5th Heavenly Stem
## (WÙ)

戊 is the *yang* stem of the 戊 *wù* 己 *jǐ* pair associated with the Earth element. In the 八字 *bā zì* horoscope system its characteristics are of steadiness, loyalty and dependability. However, steadfastness can turn into stubbornness and the inability to think quickly or easily change a chosen course can lead to difficulties.

# 6th Heavenly Stem
## (JǏ)

己 is the *yin* stem of the 戊 *wù* 己 *jǐ* pair associated with the Earth element. In the 八字 *bā zì* horoscope system its characteristics are of caring and resourcefulness. Loyalty is an enduring quality, but, unusually for a *yin–yang* combination 己 shares its pair's inability to make swift decisions or change a chosen course of action.

# 7th Heavenly Stem
### (GĒNG)

庚 is the *yang* stem of the 庚 *gēng* 辛 *xīn* pair associated with the
Metal element. In the 八字 *bā zì* horoscope system its characteristics
are of stamina and durability, as befits a Metal stem. Endurance
in pursuit of a worthwhile goal or in support of friendship is a key
quality, but it can be counter-balanced by inflexibility.

# 8th Heavenly Stem
## (XĪN)

辛 is the *yin* stem of the 庚 *gēng* 辛 *xīn* pair associated with the Metal element. In the 八字 *bā zì* horoscope system its characteristics may perhaps be seen as more negative than most of the other stems. It values face and recognition above all, and while it may be drawn into loyalty, even sentimentality, it is loath to take second place.

# 9th Heavenly Stem
## (RÉN)

壬 is the *yang* stem of the 壬 *rén* 癸 *guǐ* pair associated with the Water element. In the 八字 *bā zì* horoscope system its characteristics are, like its element, restless, adaptable and extrovert. Craving action and adventure, it can move mountains but it can be hampered by rebelliousness and the need to stand out from the ordinary.

# 10th Heavenly Stem
## (GUǏ)

癸 is the *yin* stem of the 壬 *rén* 癸 *guǐ* pair associated with the Water element. In the 八字 *bā zì* horoscope system it shares some watery characteristics with its *yang* pair, particularly in its restlessness. It is, however, introvert to 壬's extrovert, and is more principled and supportive. It is creative and supportive but may lack staying power.

# Associated Vocabulary

(YǑU LIÁN CÍ HUÌ)

# Horoscope

## (ZHĀN XĪNG)

占星 literally means 'to observe the stars', and by adding either the character 學 *xué* (study) or 術 *shù* (method, technique) you obtain the commonest Chinese terms for astrology. Astronomy is called 天文 *tiān wén*, the language of the heavens. The foundations of the systems of Chinese astrology that we know today were laid down in the Bronze Age, and there is evidence that points to some traditions already in existence in Neolithic times. Knowing the will of heaven was essential to Chinese emperors to justify their rule.

# To Be Born In The Year Of…
## (SHǓ)

属 is a particularly Chinese Chinese character. A quick dictionary
search will give, as well as the above, several meanings including
category, genus, family member, subordinate and to constitute.
Its most useful function, however, is as an indirect way of asking
someone's age. By enquiring what zodiac animal a person was born
under, the 12-year cycle means that you can tell which year they were
born in – as long as their appearance is not unusually youthful or
prematurely old for their actual age.

# Yīn Yáng

You will notice that the left-hand side of the two characters 陰 *yīn* and 陽 *yáng* are the same. This symbol is the part of the character called the radical, which gives the underlying category of meaning of the whole. In this case it is the 'hill' radical, and the right-hand sides of each, known somewhat misleadingly as the phonetic, are 'cloudy' and 'bright' respectively. Thus the fundamental duality of the *yin–yang* principle is vividly illustrated in the very way it is written as the two sides of a hill in sunshine.

# The Eight Characters
## (BĀ ZÌ)

八字 is short for 生辰八字 *shēng chēn bā zì* literally 'birth time eight characters'. These eight characters form the 四柱命理 *sì zhù mìng lǐ* or four Pillars of Life. The four Pillars are the year, month, day and hour of your birth from which astrologers can calculate your destiny. Each pillar is represented by a two-character combination of Heavenly Stem and Earthly Branch, giving a total of 八字 – eight characters.

# Daoism
## (DÀO JIÀO)

Daoism (also written Taoism, but 'D' gives the correct pronunciation) is the native Chinese philosophy/religion from which Chinese astrology draws much of its theoretical base. The canonical text of Daoism is 道德经 *Dào Dé Jīng*, literally the classic of the way of virtue, which is traditionally held to have been written by 老子 *Lǎozi* sometime around the sixth century BC. Daoism remains the second most popular religion practised in China after Buddhism, with which it has a natural affinity.

# Chinese Zodiac Chart

| Rat | 1912 | 1924 | 1936 | 1948 | 1960 | 1972 | 1984 | 1996 | 2008 |
|---|---|---|---|---|---|---|---|---|---|
| **Ox** | 1913 | 1925 | 1937 | 1949 | 1961 | 1973 | 1985 | 1997 | 2009 |
| **Tiger** | 1914 | 1926 | 1938 | 1950 | 1962 | 1974 | 1986 | 1998 | 2010 |
| **Rabbit** | 1915 | 1927 | 1939 | 1951 | 1963 | 1975 | 1987 | 1999 | 2011 |
| **Dragon** | 1916 | 1928 | 1940 | 1952 | 1964 | 1976 | 1988 | 2000 | 2012 |
| **Snake** | 1917 | 1929 | 1941 | 1953 | 1965 | 1977 | 1989 | 2001 | 2013 |
| **Horse** | 1918 | 1930 | 1942 | 1954 | 1966 | 1978 | 1990 | 2002 | 2014 |
| **Sheep** | 1919 | 1931 | 1943 | 1955 | 1967 | 1979 | 1991 | 2003 | 2015 |
| **Monkey** | 1920 | 1932 | 1944 | 1956 | 1968 | 1980 | 1992 | 2004 | 2016 |
| **Rooster** | 1921 | 1933 | 1945 | 1957 | 1969 | 1981 | 1993 | 2005 | 2017 |
| **Dog** | 1922 | 1934 | 1946 | 1958 | 1970 | 1982 | 1994 | 2006 | 2018 |
| **Pig** | 1923 | 1935 | 1947 | 1959 | 1971 | 1983 | 1995 | 2007 | 2019 |

The precise origins of the twelve animals of the Chinese zodiac are obscure, but they date back to at least the third–second century BC. There are twelve because the ancient calendar was based around the orbit of the planet Jupiter which takes 12 years (11.86 according to modern astronomy). The twelve divisions are used not just for the cycle of the years, but to represent the months and the 12 two hour divisions that made up the day. The significance of the animals is still very influential in Chinese communities today, and has a measurable effect on matters as diverse as the birth-rate and commercial investment.

# The 24 Cardinal Directions

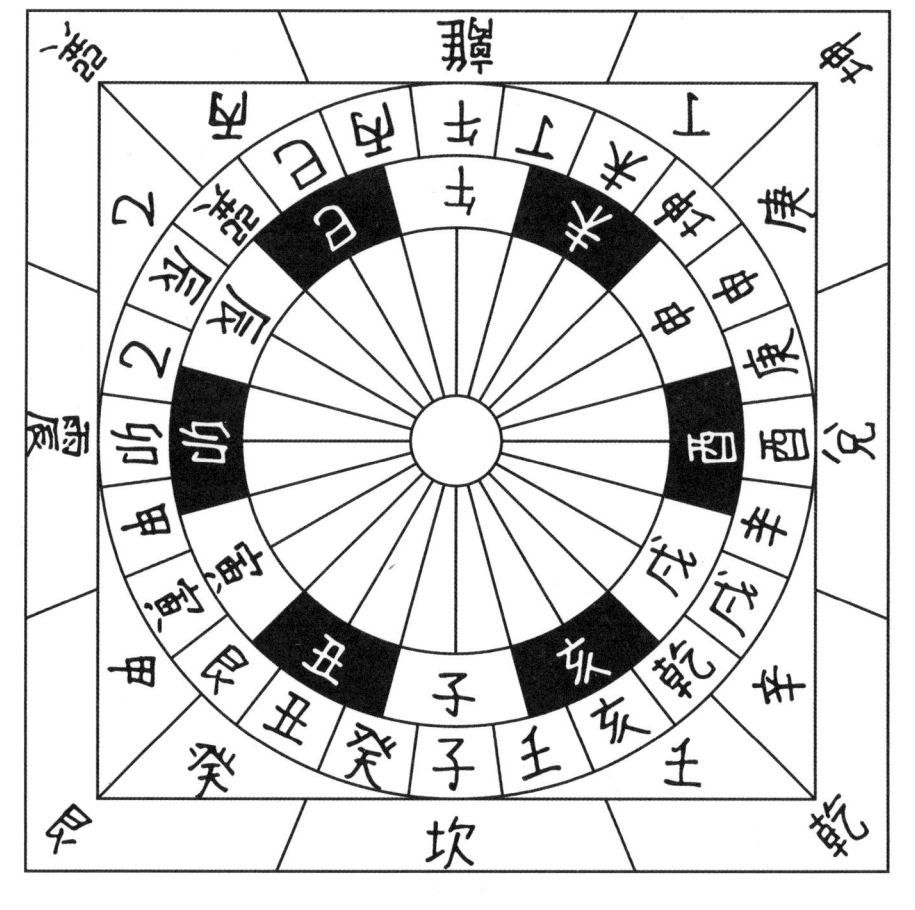

The four Cardinal Directions further divided into the 28 Celestial mansions, sub-divisions of the passage of the Moon related to the constellations. Each of the four directions is represented by a Celestial Guardian: the Green or Azure Dragon of the East, the Black Tortoise of the North, the White Tiger of the West and the Vermilion Bird of the South. They are central to traditional Chinese astronomy, astrology and geomancy (*feng shui*).

# Index